Science in a Flash

Electricity

Georgia
Amson-Bradshaw

W
FRANKLIN WATTS
LONDON•SYDNEY

Franklin Watts
First published in Great Britain in 2017 by The Watts Publishing Group

Copyright © The Watts Publishing Group 2017

Produced for Franklin Watts by
White-Thomson Publishing Ltd
www.wtpub.co.uk

Credits
Series Editor: Georgia Amson-Bradshaw
Series Designer: Rocket Design (East Anglia) Ltd

Images from Shutterstock.com: BlueRingMedia 6l, Verena Matthew Missing 7l, Vasin Lee 7t,
Eric Isselee 10bl, Stokkete 11tl, nito 16l, cyo bo 18b, MiMaLeFi 19c, jagoda 20br, Dream Master 23,
littleartvector 24cr, 25c, Iconic Bestiary 25b, Volodymyr Krasyuk 26tc
Images from other sources: UniEnergy Technologies 16c, Wellcome Images 16bc,
Tennessee Valley Authority 20
Illustrations by Steve Evans: 6b, 7br, 11br, 13b, 17br, 18cr, 19br, 20bl, 27r
All design elements from Shutterstock.

Every attempt has been made to clear copyright. Should there be any inadvertent omission
please apply to the publisher for rectification.

HB ISBN 978 1 4451 5270 7
PB ISBN 978 1 4451 5271 4

Printed in China

MIX
Paper from
responsible sources
FSC® C104740
www.fsc.org

Franklin Watts
An imprint of
Hachette Children's Group
Part of The Watts Publishing Group
Carmelite House
50 Victoria Embankment
London EC4Y 0DZ

An Hachette UK Company
www.hachette.co.uk

www.franklinwatts.co.uk

WARNING
Never cut or damage the
cables of electrical items,
and never stick anything
into plug sockets.

Contents

WHAT IS ELECTRICITY?

Electricity is a type of energy generated by the movement of electrons.

Energy is the ability to do 'work', to make things happen. Electrical energy is a type of energy, and we use it to power many of our appliances such as lightbulbs, televisions and fridges. Electrical energy is generated by the movement of **electrons**.

It's all about the atoms

Everything in the universe is made up of **atoms**, which are the unimaginably tiny building blocks that make all stuff. But atoms themselves are made up of even smaller bits, called **neutrons, protons** and electrons. Each of these bits or 'particles' have a different **charge**.

This is great!

No it's not!

Meh...

Protons have a positive charge.

Electrons have a negative charge.

Neutrons are neutral, they have no charge.

Moody atoms?

Of course, positive and negative charge aren't anything to do with the atom being in a good or a bad mood! It's similar to the forces in a magnet. Magnets have a north pole and a south pole. Opposite poles attract one another. It's the same with protons and electrons: positively and negatively charged particles are attracted to one another.

Whizzy electrons

Unlike protons and neutrons, which huddle together in the middle and hold on tightly to each other, electrons whizz around the outside of atoms. Because of this, they are more easily separated from the rest of the atom.

Electrons on the move

When an atom has an even number of protons and electrons, it has no electrical charge. But if some of the electrons are 'knocked off', or if more electrons are added, it gives the atom an electrical charge. As electrons move around from atom to atom, they carry electrical energy.

An electron hops from one atom to another, giving the atoms electrical charge.

EYE SPY!

How many electrons can you count?

Where does ELECTRICITY come from?

Electricity occurs in nature as well as being generated by humans.

Although we think of electricity mainly as being quite modern technology, electricity occurs naturally. In fact – there is electrical energy moving around inside your body right now!

You've got nerve

Your brain communicates with the rest of your body through your nervous system; your body's information highway. Signals travel from your senses to your brain, and instructions travel from your brain to your muscles along your nerve network. These signals are made of tiny bursts of electricity, so without electricity your body wouldn't work at all.

Shocking behaviour!

Electrical attack

Other animals use electricity in more dramatic ways, such as the electric eel that sends out high voltage blasts to stun and kill prey. Their bodies contain special cells that store electricty like tiny batteries.

Dangerous nature

One of the most powerful natural occurrences of electricity is lightning. Lightning is very powerful, and can destroy buildings and kill animals. It is caused when ice crystals inside storm clouds rub against each other, exchanging electrons and building up electrical charge. When the charge gets big enough, it connects with positively charged particles on the ground in a bolt of lightning.

Man-made electricity

Although lightning is incredibly powerful, we cannot capture it and use it to power our homes. The electicity we use on a daily basis is instead made or 'generated' in power plants, or by renewable technologies such as solar panels. Read more about power generation on page 20.

POP QUIZ!

Which of these uses electricity to move and think?
Answer on page 28.

a) a human   b) a robot

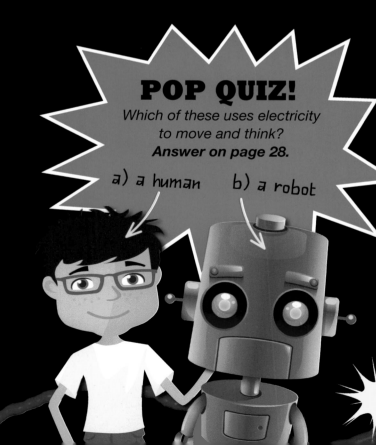

7

What do we use

We use electricity for lighting, heating, transport, communication and travel.

Have you ever had a power cut at home? The TV goes off and the lights go out. Power cuts can be kind of exciting at first because they don't happen often. But imagine if life was like that all the time. Everything would be much more difficult without lights, entertainment, electric tools and heating.

At home

Electricity lights and often heats our homes. It powers our washing machines and dishwashers, and our fridges and freezers. Without electricity all washing would have to be done by hand, and food would quickly go off. There would be no television to watch or computer games to play.

Transport

Many trains that take people to and from work run on electricity. Without trains, more people would have to live closer to their workplace. Our cities would have to be organised very differently.

electricity for?

Communication

Without electricity there would be no telephones or Internet. You couldn't communicate with people who lived far away unless you sent them a letter. You couldn't use the Internet to do your homework.

Making stuff

Electricity drives the machines in factories that make the objects we use, the clothes we wear, or that process the food we eat. Everything would need to be made by hand, and so would be much more expensive and hard to get.

FACT ATTACK

A bright start

The first commercially successful electric lightbulb was developed and sold by Thomas Edison in the 1870s.

All about STATIC electricity

A material that has gained or lost electrons becomes charged with static electricity.

We already know that electricity is to do with whizzy electrons moving between atoms. But there are two types of electricity, **static electricity**, and **current** electricity. So what's the difference?

Electron imbalance

Static electricity occurs when electrical energy gathers in one place because a material has lost or gained extra electrons. A material that has lost some of its electrons has a positive charge. A material that has gained extra electrons has a negative charge.

Help me please ... my owners have no fashion sense!

Static electricity is often produced by rubbing materials together, such as if you rub a balloon on a woollen jumper. Some of the electrons from the balloon get transferred onto the jumper, leaving the balloon with a positive charge, and the jumper with a negative one.

Opposites attract

Objects with opposite charges will attract, so a negatively charged balloon will cling to a positively charged jumper.

Hey girl ... my positively charged jumper is attracted to your negatively charged balloon...

Cringe!

Give it a go!

Can you make a remote controlled drinks can?

Find an empty drinks can and a balloon. Inflate the balloon and rub it on your hair or a woollen jumper to charge it with static electricity.

Lay the can on its side on a flat surface. Hold the balloon about 2 cm away from the side of the can. The can should start to roll towards the balloon.

Slowly move the balloon away from the can. How far and how fast can you make the can follow the balloon?

Why does the can roll at all? **Read more on page 28.**

Electrical current and circuits

Electrical energy flows around circuits.

Current electricity is electricity that moves around, and is the sort of electricity we use to power our machines and appliances. Current electricity is carried by electrons moving between atoms, but in order for a current to happen, you need a **circuit**.

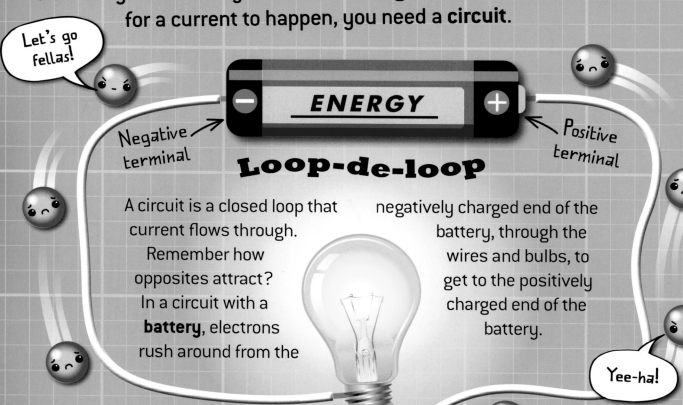

Let's go fellas!

Negative terminal

ENERGY

Positive terminal

Loop-de-loop

A circuit is a closed loop that current flows through. Remember how opposites attract? In a circuit with a **battery**, electrons rush around from the negatively charged end of the battery, through the wires and bulbs, to get to the positively charged end of the battery.

Yee-ha!

Hardworking electrons

The energetic little electrons 'work' as they flow along the route of the circuit, lighting up a bulb or driving a motor as they pass, similar to how a flow of water drives a waterwheel.

Road ahead closed

If you break the loop of a circuit, electricity stops flowing, as the electrons are no longer being attracted to the other side of the circuit. Breaking the loop is what a switch does.

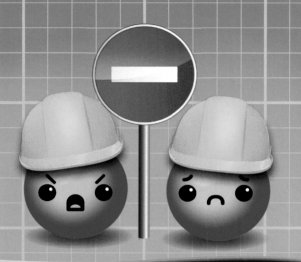

Give it a go!

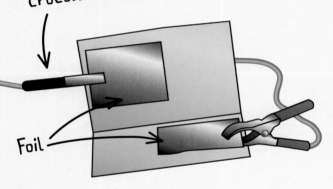

crocodile clips

Foil

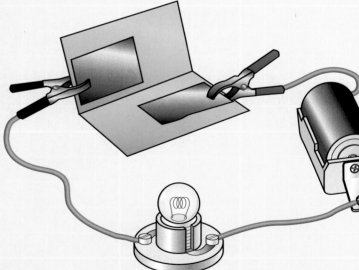

See a circuit with a switch in action. You will need three wires with crocodile clips, a battery with a holder, a lightbulb with a holder, a piece of thin card folded in half, a glue stick and some aluminium foil.

First make your switch. Glue pieces of aluminium foil onto the inside of your folded piece of card, so that when the card is open they don't touch, but shutting the card touches the foil together.

Clip a wire with a crocodile clip onto each side of the card, so that the metal clips are touching the foil.

Create a circuit with your battery, bulb, and switch like this. Fold the card closed to complete the circuit, and open the card to break it.

WARNING
NEVER use mains electricity for experiments: it is powerful enough to kill!

CONDUCTORS AND INSULATORS

Electricity can only pass through certain materials, called conductors.

There is a good reason your parents tell you never to stick things in the plug sockets. Electricity can be very dangerous, and the power running through the wires in your house is strong enough to kill. But if electricty is so strong, why don't we get zapped all the time?

Protective barrier

One of the key reasons it is safe to use electrical appliances is because not every type of material will carry electrical current. The ones that do are called **conductors**, and the ones that don't are called **insulators**. The cables of our appliances are always covered in thick rubber that electricity cannot pass through. This stops us getting shocked when we touch them.

Rubber covers the wires on our devices.

Conductors and insulators

Metals are the best conductors. Salt water and pencil lead (which is actually called 'graphite') are also conductors, although they are not as efficient. Plastic, paper, wood, rubber, wool and glass are all good insulators. They do not let electricity pass.

No, I'M the best conductor!

It's all about the atoms

Some conductors also carry electricity more easily than others. Whether a material is a good conductor or not is all down to the atoms the material is made from. The atoms of some materials hold their electrons very tightly, so it's hard for the electrons to get passed between atoms and carry electrical charge.

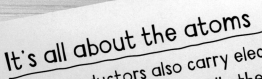

Other types of atom have 'looser' electrons, which can travel between atoms more freely. Materials made of these types of atom conduct electricity better. Most metals are good at carrying electrical current.

Fizzy drink

Plastic ruler

Rubber

Pencil lead

Metal paper clips

POP QUIZ!

Which of these objects are conductors, and which are insulators?
Answer on page 28.

Woolly sock

All about BATTERIES

A battery is a device used to store electrical energy.

We know that the electricity needs to flow around a circuit to work. But what do you do when you need to store electricity? You use a battery.

All shapes and sizes

All sorts of batteries exist, from tiny little discs in a wristwatch, to huge, building-sized battery complexes that are used as back-ups in some towns in case the normal electricity supply fails.

FACT ATTACK

Battery man

In 1800 Alessandro Volta discovered that a stack of zinc and copper discs separated by leather discs soaked in salt water generated an electrical current. He had invented the first battery.

Large numbers of big batteries like these are often used alongside renewable energy technologies like solar panels, to store power to use when the sun isn't shining.

Awesome! But how will I fit it in the TV remote?

3v

Battery 1.5v

-ion AAA

AAA

Battery 1.5v

Cool chemicals

Batteries have three main parts, a positive terminal, a negative terminal, and a chemical called the **electrolyte** that separates them.

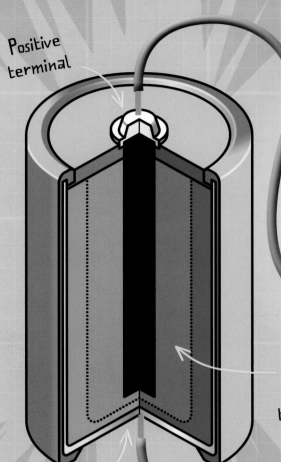

Positive terminal

Chemical reactions take place in the electrolyte

Negative terminal

When a battery is hooked up to a circuit, chemical reactions in the electrolyte take place that make electrons build up at the negative terminal. The electrons then flow around the circuit, powering devices. These chemical reactions turn the electrolyte into new chemicals. Eventually, all the chemicals are changed, and the battery no longer has energy.

EYE SPY!
How many batteries can you count?

Riddle me this!

A boy puts new batteries in his torch, but the bulb won't come on. So he changes the bulb. It still won't turn on. What's the problem? Answer on page 29.

17

ELECTRICITY AND MAGNETISM

Electricity passing through a wire generates a magnetic field.

Early scientists investigating electricity discovered the links between electricity and magnetism, when a wire carrying electricity was put near a compass. The compass needle moved, showing that the electricity in the wire was generating a magnetic field.

It moved, it moved!

Super strength

The discovery that an electric current creates a magnetic field led on to the development of **electromagnets**. Electromagnets are super powerful magnets made of wire coiled round an iron core. They are only magnetic when electricity is flowing through the wire. Electromagnets are very, very strong, and are used in many ways. They lift large amounts of scrap metal in scrap yards, and can even hold entire trains in the air!

In a spin

Electromagnetism can also power electric motors, which make things spin round and round. They are found inside washing machines, or remote-controlled cars. They work by putting an electromagnet next to a permanent magnet. When the electromagnet is turned on, the two magnets repel one another, and this repelling force is used to drive an axle round at high speed.

Yep, like I thought, the motor's gone. That's gonna cost ya!

Make your very own electromagnet! You'll need a large iron nail, about one metre of thin coated copper wire, some paper clips, some electrical tape and a D size battery.

1. Leaving about 15cm of wire at one end, bind the copper wire tightly around the nail. Wrap the wire neatly around and don't overlap them.

2. Cut the wire so that there is a 15cm length at the other end too. Strip the coating off the ends of the wire so the copper is exposed. Using the electrical tape, secure the wires to either end of the battery. Be careful as the wire can get hot.

3. Your nail is now an electromagnet! Try picking up the paperclips with the end of the nail.

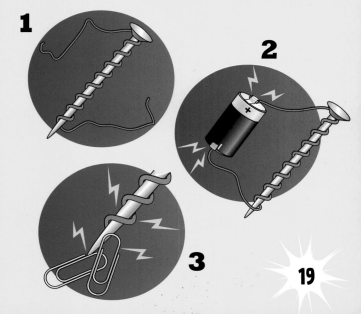

1

2

3

How do we make

The electricity that comes out of the sockets in our homes is mostly made, or 'generated', in power stations. Just like you can't make a cake without ingredients, energy can't be created from nothing. It has to be turned from one type of energy to another. There are different types of power station, but they make electricity in basically the same way – see the steps 1–3 here.

1

Chemical to electrical

Energy from another source, such as coal or natural gas is changed into electrical energy in a power station.

Did you know?

Methane gas from cow poo can be burnt in power stations to produce electricity.

Tooot!

ELECTRICITY?

2

Fuel makes steam

Inside the power station, the fuel is burnt, heating water in a boiler and turning it into steam.

Spinning wire coil

Movement and magnets

Just as electricity running through a coil of wire generates a magnetic field, this works in reverse: a coil of wire being spun past a magnet makes an electrical current flow through the wire.

3

Steam turns a turbine

The steam drives a turbine (like a fan). The circular rotation of the turbine is what drives the **generator**. Inside the generator coiled wire is spun very fast past a strong magnet. This makes electrical current flow through the wire, and it is this electrical current which travels along cables to our homes.

All about
RENEWABLE ENERGY

Power from wind, water, the Sun and the earth can be used to make electricity.

Most of the electricity that powers our homes is generated in power plants that burn **fossil fuels**, such as coal and natural gas. But burning fossil fuels has big downsides. For one, they aren't renewable – which means they will eventually run out. They also release a gas called carbon dioxide into the air, which causes **climate change**. However, fossil fuels aren't the only way to turn generators...

Water power

Instead of steam, **hydroelectric** power stations use water flowing through rivers to spin the generators.

Here comes the Sun

Another way of generating electricity is to use **solar power**. This method does not produce electricity by spinning magnets inside metal coils. It uses 'photovoltaic cells' made of specially treated silicon, which capture light energy from the Sun. The silicon cells can use the Sun's energy to push electrons around a circuit.

Riddle me this!

Sun and wind are excellent free sources of energy. But the Sun doesn't always shine, and the wind doesn't always blow. How could people solve this problem?

Answer on page 29.

Blow wind blow

In the past people used windmills to grind corn for flour. Nowadays, windmills can generate electricity.

Hot rocks

In some parts of the world, we can power turbines using **geothermal** energy. This captures heat from volcanic activity underneath the surface of the Earth to boil water and create steam.

FACT ATTACK

Old bones

Fossil fuels such as oil and coal are made from the remains of plants and animals that lived millions of years ago.

HOW DO WE MEASURE ELECTRICITY?

Volts measure the strength of an electricity source; amps measure the flow of electrical current.

If you look at a normal battery that you can buy in the supermarket, you will see somewhere on it a number like this: 1.5V. The letter V stands for **volts**, which is the unit of measurement we use to describe the strength of a power source.

HOME FARM WATER

Volts = force not flow

Volts do not measure the current, or the amount of electricity flowing through a circuit. The amount of current flowing through a circuit is measured in amps. So what ARE volts? It might all seem a bit confusing, but it's simple if you think about it like water, as shown in examples 1 and 2 here.

1

Imagine a big tank of water with a thin hose coming out the bottom. The water is being pushed out through the hose by the pressure of the water. The pushing power of the water in the tank is like the voltage. How much water is flowing through the hose is like the current (measured in amps).

Now it all makes sense!

Understanding CIRCUITS

More volts in a circuit means more 'push' to power a device.

Circuits can be very simple, or they can be very complicated. However big or small your circuit, each part of a circuit has a job.

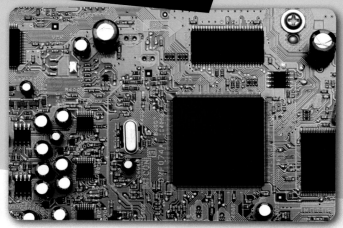

Drawing circuits

Electrical circuits like the ones inside your computers and smart phones can be incredibly complicated. So when scientists and engineers are designing and working with circuits, it helps to have a diagram that can show all the different parts clearly and simply.

The symbols

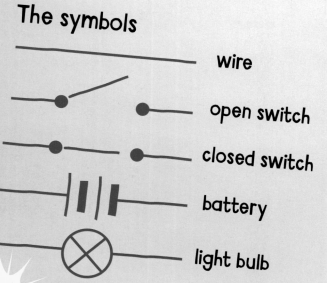

wire

open switch

closed switch

battery

light bulb

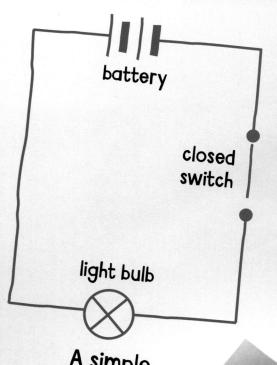

battery

closed switch

light bulb

A simple circuit diagram

Bright bulbs, dim bulbs

In an electrical circuit, just like in life, the more work there is to be done, the more energy you need! In a simple circuit of batteries, wires and light bulbs, lighting up the bulbs is the work that the electrical energy is doing.

Give it a go!

Investigate the effect that adding and removing batteries from a circuit has on the brightness of two bulbs. You will need two bulbs with holders, two AA batteries with holders, and four wires with crocodile clips.

Set up a circuit with two bulbs and one battery. How brightly do the bulbs glow?

Now, add a second battery to the circuit, next to the first one. Make sure that the positive end of the first battery is next to the negative end of the second.

What do you notice about the brightness of the bulbs?

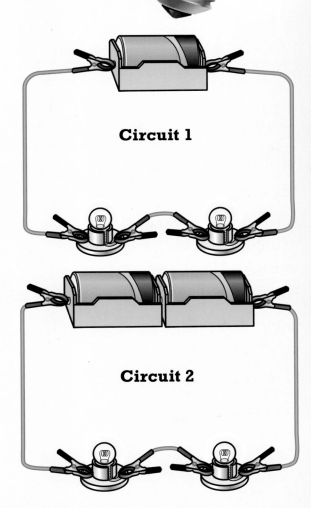

Circuit 1

Circuit 2

What's happening

If you add several bulbs to a circuit with only one battery, each bulb will glow dimly, because it's harder work for the electricity to get around the circuit. But adding more batteries to a circuit adds more voltage, or pushing power. This extra pushing power means the electricity can whizz around the circuit and light the bulbs brightly.

And the answer is ...

Page 5

Eye spy: There are 11 electrons on pages 4 and 5.

Page 7

Pop quiz: Trick question! Both a human AND a robot use electricity to move and 'think'.

Page 11

Give it a go: The can rolls because the extra electrons in the negatively-charged balloon repel the electrons in the neutrally-charged can (remember opposite charges attract, and similar charges repel, like magnets). Because electrons can move around easily, the side of the can next to the balloon is left with more protons than electrons. This means that part of the can is now positively charged, and so it rolls towards the negatively-charged balloon.

Page 15

Pop quiz: The metal paper clips, the pencil lead and the fizzy drink are all conductors (only the liquid of the drink though, not the glass). The woolly sock, the rubber and the plastic ruler are all insulators.

Page 17

Riddle me this: If a torch won't light when the batteries and the bulb are new, the batteries might be the wrong way round, or there must be a break in the circuit somewhere.

Page 17

Eye Spy: There are 14 batteries on pages 16 and 17 (not including photographs).

Page 23

Riddle me this: Renewable energy from wind and the Sun are great, except when the Sun isn't shining and the wind isn't blowing! So people get around this by having huge battery complexes (like the type shown on page 16). These building-sized batteries can store extra electricity generated when the Sun is shining brightly or the wind is blowing hard, ready to flow into the mains when the solar panels or wind turbines aren't generating electricity.

Page 25

Pop quiz: The answer is A, voltage measures the pushing power of an electricity source. In a circuit, it is hard work for the little electrons to push through devices such as bulbs or motors. The stronger the pushing power from the battery or electricity source, the brighter the bulb can glow.

Glossary

Amps A measurment of the flow of current through a circuit

Atoms Tiny building blocks that everything in the universe is made of

Battery A storage device that can supply electrical energy to a circuit

Charge The balance of protons and electrons in an atom or material

Circuit A loop that electricity flows around

Climate change Changes in the weather around the world due to global warming

Conductor A material that lets electrical current flow through it

Current The flow of electrons round a circuit

Electrolyte The chemical mixture inside a battery that produces charge

Electromagnet A powerful magnet that is only magnetic when an electrical current is running past

Electron One of the tiny bits that make up an atom

Fossil fuel A type of non-renewable fuel such as coal or oil taken out of the ground

Generator A machine that spins a metal coil past a magnet to produce electricity

Geothermal energy Electricity produced using the heat of volcanic activity underground

Hydroelectric energy Electricity produced using the power of water flowing through turbines

Insulator A material that does not let electrical current flow through it

Negative charge When a material or atom has more electrons than protons

Neutron One of the tiny bits that make up an atom

Positive charge When a material or atom has more protons than electrons

Proton One of the tiny bits that make up an atom

Solar power Electricity generated from the Sun's energy

Static electricity Electricity that builds in one place and does not flow

Volts The pushing power of an electricity source

Further reading

Electric Shocks: Disgusting and Dreadful Science
Anna Claybourne (Franklin Watts, 2014)

**Spark! Electricity and how it
works:** The Real Scientist
Peter Riley (Franklin Watts, 2012)

Electricity and Magnets: Mind Webs
Anna Claybourne (Wayland, 2014)

Electricity: Amazing Science
Sally Hewitt (Wayland, 2014)

Websites

www.switchedonkids.org.uk/
A website full of games, quizzes and learning about electricity.

www.bbc.co.uk/education/topics/zj44jxs
Video clips all about electricity.

www.exploratorium.edu/snacks/subject/electricity-and-magnetism
Fun experiments to do at home.

www.explainthatstuff.com/electricity.html
Detailed information about electricity.

Index

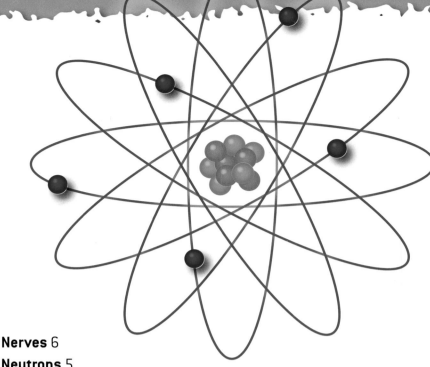